THE COMMON SALVATION

The Book of Jude Unlocked Through Kabbalah

For My Parents

Louis & Evelyn Goldstein

Thank you for life

ISBN-13: 978-0692231005
ISBN-10: 0692231005

The Common Salvation
Sheila R. Vitale

Requests for permission to reproduce selections
from this book should be mailed to:

Christ-Centered Kabbalah
Sheila R. Vitale
P O Box 562
Port Jefferson Station, NY 11776-0562
(631) 331-1493

Table of Authorities

1. **Brown Driver & Briggs' Hebrew Lexicon**, Woodside Bible Fellowship, Ontario, Canada, Licensed From The Institute for Creation Research.

2. **Englishman's Greek-Hebrew Concordance**.

3. **Gesenius' Hebrew and Chaldee Lexicon to the Old Testament** Scriptures, Baker Book House, Grand Rapids, Michigan.

4. **The Interlinear Bible** (Jay P. Green, Sr.), Hendrickson Publisher's, Peabody, Massachusetts 01961-3473.

5. **The Interlinear Bible (transliterated), Biblesoft and International Bible Translators, Inc**.

6. **Nave's Topical Bible**.

7. **Nelson's Bible Dictionary**, Thomas Nelson, Inc., Publishers, Nashville, Tennessee.

8. **Strong's Exhaustive Concordance** (James Strong) Thomas Nelson, Inc., Publishers, Nashville, Tennessee.

9. **Strong's Hebrew And Chaldee Dictionary** (James Strong), Thomas Nelson, Inc., Publishers, Nashville, Tennessee.

10. **Strong's Greek Dictionary** (James Strong), Thomas Nelson, Inc., Publishers, Nashville, Tennessee.

11. **The New Thayer's Greek-English Lexicon Of The New Testament**, Hendrickson Publisher's, Peabody, Massachusetts 01961-3473.

12.   **Unger's Bible Dictionary** (Merrill F. Unger), The Moody Bible Institute of Chicago, Chicago, Illinois 60610.

13.   **1979 Authorized Version** (AV), The On-Line Bible

14.   **Stephanus Greek Text**, The On-Line Bible

15.   **Green's Literal Translation**, The On-Line Bible

Christ-Centered Kabbalah

Sheila R. Vitale
Pastor, Teacher, Founder
PO Box 562
Port Jefferson Station, NY 11776 USA

THE COMMON SALVATION

**Edited and Adapted as a Book by
Sheila R. Vitale**

THE COMMON SALVATION

Formatted as a Book by
The CCK Professional Software Specialist Staff

Christ-Centered Kabbalah

~ The Compleat Kabbalah ~

Sheila R. Vitale
Pastor, Teacher & Founder

Ministry Staff
Anthony Milton, Teacher (South Carolina)
Brooke Paige, Teacher (New York)
Sandra Aldrich (MN) (July 7, 1975 – April 18, 2021)

Administrative Staff
Susan Panebianco, Office Manager

Editorial Staff
Rose Herczeg, Editor

Technical Staff
Lape Mobolaji-Lawal, Database Administrator

Ministry Illustrators
Cecilia H. Bryant (Oct. 18, 1921 – Oct. 23, 2013)
Fidelis Onwubueke

Music Staff
June Eble, Singer, Lyricist and Clarinetist
(July 20, 1931 – Jan. 24, 2024)
Don Gervais, Singer, Lyricist and Guitarist
Rita L. Rora, Singer, Lyricist and Guitarist

Table of Contents

The Alternate Translation Bible©

The Alternate Translation Bible (**ATB**) is an original translation of the Scripture.

Alternate Translation of the Old Testament©
Alternate Translation, Exodus, Chapter 32
 (Crime of the Calf)©
Alternate Translation, Daniel, Chapter 8©
Alternate Translation, Daniel, Chapter 11©
Alternate Translation, Genesis 9:18-27
 (The Noah Chronicles, Second Edition) ©

Alternate Translation of the New Testament©
Alternate Translation, 2 Thessalonians, Chapter 2
 (Sophia)©
Alternate Translation, 1st John, Chapter 5©
Alternate Translation, the Book of Colossians
 (To The Church At Colosse) ©
Alternate Translation, the Book of Corinthians, Chapter 11
 (Corinthian Confusion) ©
Alternate Translation, the Book of Jude
 (The Common Salvation)©

Alternate Translation of the Book of the Revelation of Jesus
 Christ to St. John©
Traducción Alternada del Libro de Revelación de Jesucristo©

Christ-Centered Kabbalah

Sheila R. Vitale

Pastor, Teacher, Founder

PO Box 562

Port Jefferson Station, NY 11776 USA

THE COMMON SALVATION

Translated, Edited and Compiled by
Sheila R. Vitale

THE BOOK OF JUDE

PREFACE

Preface

The core of Jude's Message is that ***the Common Salvation*** (vs 3 KJV) is the salvation of the human spirit only.

The Common Salvation **is not** the atonement that saves the personality.

Rom 5:11
AND NOT ONLY SO, BUT WE ALSO JOY IN GOD THROUGH OUR LORD JESUS CHRIST, BY WHOM WE HAVE NOW RECEIVED THE ATONEMENT. **KJV**

Christ Jesus,[1] the only Mediator between God and man, is the atonement that saves the personality.

1 Tim 2:5
5 FOR THERE IS ONE GOD, AND ONE MEDIATOR BETWEEN GOD AND MEN, THE MAN CHRIST JESUS; **KJV**

Jude tells us that Christ Jesus must be built up within the consciousness of the individual believer for the personality to be saved (vs 20).

1 Cor 3:10
10 ACCORDING TO THE GRACE OF GOD WHICH IS GIVEN UNTO ME, AS A WISE MASTERBUILDER, I HAVE LAID THE FOUNDATION, AND ANOTHER BUILDETH THEREON. BUT LET EVERY MAN TAKE HEED HOW HE BUILDETH THEREUPON. **KJV**

---

[1] **Christ Jesus is the New Testament name for the female Adam, the righteous personality of mankind.**

Then, Jude goes on to warn us about the fallen kings[2] hidden in the unconscious part of the mind (vs 12-13),

2 Peter 2:4

4 FOR IF GOD SPARED NOT THE ANGELS THAT SINNED, BUT CAST THEM DOWN TO HELL, AND DELIVERED THEM INTO CHAINS OF DARKNESS, TO BE RESERVED UNTO JUDGMENT; **KJV**

and, finally,

Jude declares that the Spirit of Truth must be separated (vs 19, 22) from the bestial nature through the exposure of hidden sin (vs 14-15, 25), for the personality to be saved.

Heb 4:12

12 FOR THE WORD OF GOD IS QUICK, AND POWERFUL, AND SHARPER THAN ANY TWOEDGED SWORD, PIERCING EVEN TO THE DIVIDING ASUNDER OF SOUL AND SPIRIT, AND OF THE JOINTS AND MARROW, AND IS A DISCERNER OF THE THOUGHTS AND INTENTS OF THE HEART. **KJV**

Sheila R. Vitale,

Translator

---

2 *Angels* are called *kings* when they are revealed through the mind of a man.

THE BOOK OF JUDE

INTRODUCTION

Introduction

Preparing To Translate

The Common Salvation, An Exposition on the Alternate Translation of the Book of Jude.

Three Hebrew-English dictionaries, three Interlinear Texts, and multiple Bible Dictionaries (see, Table of Authorities at the beginning of this book), as well as online English dictionaries, encyclopedias and search engines, were used to search out the meaning of each Greek word of the Book of Jude, and to acquire as much information as possible about obviously, and not so obviously related topics, that are revealed through the *Alternate Translation.*

In addition, each word and verse was seriously prayed about in an attempt to discover God's spiritual message behind the written words.

The Alternate Translation of the Book of Jude, contains Translators Notes and Comments, that explain the spiritual principles revealed and discussed in the Alternate Translations. In addition, there is a Table of References that lists all of the Scriptures mentioned in the Book.

It is not unusual for the verse structure of the *Alternate Translations* to be rearranged so that they can be read as one continuous message. Accordingly, some paragraph numbers are out of order (*3* before *2*, for example).

Alternate Translations Are Progressive

Alternate Translations are rendered for each verse in its entirety, after which all of the translated verses are read together as one whole revelation, to confirm their synchronicity, reveal additional, deep nuances of the revelation of the whole Chapter, and to expose any inconsistencies or errors.

Alternate Translations are progressive in that the *Alternate Translation* for each verse is affected by the *Alternate Translations* for previous and subsequent verses. A newly translated verse, for example will be influenced by previous Alternate Translations, and sometimes the Alternate Translation for the new verse causes changes in previously translated verses.

The Word of God Is Alive

Written words are vessels that clothe the spiritual word, just like the body is a vessel that carries the soul in this world. We might even say that the spiritual understanding of a written word is the soul of that written word.

The *Alternate Translation* of a whole chapter of Scripture is a living organism that evolves and grows in scope. Unveiling the spiritual meaning of a word shatters its hard exterior, so that the spiritual contents flow out and blend with the spiritual contents of the other shattered vessels.

The Spirit of Revelation then takes hold of the Word of God in this *liquid form* to further refine and reveal the optimal esoteric understanding of the *Alternate Translations.* In addition, the translator reads and re-reads the Alternate Translations to expose all thoughts, understanding and influences of the Carnal Mind, which would hinder the Mind of Christ from going beyond the letter of the Word.

All Alternate Translations are rendered for the benefit of a particular people, at the particular time that the Alternate Translations are rendered, as the Lord Jesus Christ leads.

Accordingly, you will find two versions of *The Alternate Translation of the Book of Jude. The Alternate Translation Work-Up (Including Translators Notes and Comments)* represent the progression of the *Alternate Translation* of the Book of Jude, from its inception to its final, annotated stage:

    1. The Alternate, Amplified Translation [ATB]

    2. The King James Version [KJV]

    3. Alternate Translation Work-Up (Including Translators Notes and Comments) [ATB]

HOW TO READ THE ALTERNATE TRANSLATION WORKUP

How To Read
The Alternate Translation Workup

Words in round parentheses ( ) are from the King James Translation.

Words in square brackets are the translator's amplifications.

Alternate translations are in blue text.

The Alternate Translations that appear in the ***work-up*** (pp 10-33) are interim translations, although the translator considered them to be final at the time they were rendered. The final translation (insofar as this book is concerned) (pp 1-6) was rendered after many prayerful considerations and reviews.

The translator's comments are in green text. They exist as a permanent record of the translator's thoughts and reasoning as she sought to comprehend what the Lord was showing her through the Book of Jude.

THE COMMON SALVATION

SALVATION

The Book of Jude Unlocked Through Kabbalah

THE BOOK OF JUDE

ALTERNATE TRANSLATION©

Alternate Translation©

1   Jude, the servant of Jesus Christ and brother of James, to [the brethren] whose [human spirit] is separated [from their bestial nature] by God the Father, and [whose personality] is preserved [through union with] Jesus Christ, and are called [to return to the immortality of innocence]:

2   May the mercy, and the peace, and the love of God be multiplied unto you.

The Reason for Writing

3   Beloved of God, it was morally necessary for me to write to you, to exhort you to seriously strive [to recover] the faith that was given to the Saints at one time; [wherefore], I have made every effort to write to you concerning the salvation that does not produce the atonement,

4   [Because], it is written that, [in the last days, the Kings] from the previous ages, who had no fear of God and were condemned by Him, shall refuse to honor our only master, the Lord Jesus Christ, and will secretly enter into [your subconscious] alongside Adam, [your righteous mind], with the intent of changing the accepted [use of your physical bodies], into vehicles [to be used] to satisfy [their] insatiable desire for [sexual] pleasure, and

5   I will, therefore, remind you of what you once knew, [that when Christ did not rise] in the people after the Lord saved them out of the land of Egypt, [their physical bodies and their personalities] were destroyed, [because there was no place for the male seed to attach itself],

Fallen Angels Punished

6   And [that] the Angels which did not guard themselves at their beginning, but left their own residences [to join with the earth], were imprisoned by the judgment [that] shackles them, [through] perpetual [reincarnations], to the dark under[side of mortal mankind], until the great day [of Jubilee, when everything will be restored to its rightful owner], and

Sodom and Gomorrah Punished

7   [That these same fallen Kings who] were separated from [Primordial Adam], their source, [and who] also came under the justice of [the Shekinah, who] burnt [them] in the [lake] of fire, are examples of [Jehovah's Sowing & Reaping Judgment upon] lust [for spiritual ascension], which corrupted the flesh of the other [species that] they were attached to, with lascivious thoughts, and

The Israel of God Punished

8   Likewise, in the same manner, [these fallen Kings], indeed, also pollute your flesh; indeed, they slander [Christ], the opinion of God, and render secular authority that promotes liberty, null and void, [to bring to pass] their dream [of a one-world Utopian society that they will rule over];

Michael Defers To The Fallen Kings

9   Indeed, when Michael, the Archangel, verbally distinguished [between] the Devil, [Moses' emotions, and Christ], Moses' living, [spiritual] body, he dared not bring an official judgment of blasphemy against [the fallen Kings within Moses], but said [to them], the Lord charges you [with blasphemy]; and

Ignorant Mankind Punished

10   As much as, indeed, the physical, irrational beasts [that] these [Kings influence] do not understand that they are speaking evil of Elohim, nevertheless, they know how to do the things that [cause Christ] to wither and shrivel up, [and enjoy them];

Warning Not To Sin

11   Woe unto them because they are following Cain's lifestyle, and making the same mistakes as Balaam, who hired out his anointing for pay, and Korah, who disputed [Moses' right to rule over Israel],

Description of The Fallen Kings

12   These [Kings] are [like] reefs in the sea [that shipwreck the souls that are born from the] love of God, so hold your [ship] on a good course, and fearlessly teach true doctrine; [and avoid] the souls that have no spirit [in their sails, but] bear up alongside [Adam to take his energy]; they are uprooted [spiritual] trees, stripped of [their outer bodies, and] unable to produce others, who died [when they left their

primordial residences, and] died again [on the other side of the flood];

14   They are gloomy shadows that wander into the unconscious part of the female mind [with] their own [interpretation of the Scripture], and guard themselves from loss or injury in this age, by incarnating as the wild, turbulent [emotions of Leviathan's male] Sefirot, [which are collectively called, the pride of man]; and

Judgment through Wisdom

14   Enoch, [the disciplinarian], the 7th [Sefirah] of Adam, prophesied of these, saying, behold, [when] the Lord comes [together with] the Saints, the wisdom

15   To judge the whole [Adam], to convince all of his souls of all [their] ungodly actions, and of all the wicked, carnal [words that their] wicked [selves] have spoken against their [righteous] selves, [is present], and

Attributes of The Fallen Kings

16   [The bodies that these fallen Kings are incarnate in], are discontented grumblers, whose mouths speak prideful [words] that flatter people for their own benefit, [whose main purpose in life is] to satisfy their own lusts;

17   Indeed, beloved, you should remember the predictions of the apostles of the Lord Jesus Christ,

18   How they told you that in the last days, there would be false teachers who would follow after their own ungodly lust [to teach, rather than the Spirit of Truth], and

19   That there would be those who would hold on to their bestial nature, and refuse to separate it from the Spirit [of Truth];

Christ Jesus Is The Atonement

20   But you, beloved of God, [who] are rearing up [Christ Jesus], the holy one, upon [the foundation of] your faith, [which you received by] praying in the Holy Spirit,

21   So, let the love of God guard you against loss or injury [in this age, rather than the raging emotions of the fallen Kings], by looking to the mercy of our Lord Jesus Christ, unto eternal life, and

Deliverance for Some

22   Have compassion on some, by thoroughly separating [their bestial nature from the Spirit of Truth], and

23   Save others by pulling them out of the fire; indeed, be compassionate, but take care that you do not stain the flesh of your body [when you draw near to] that which is detestable;

Acknowledgment of The Power of God

24 a   [Because of your] exuberant joy [over their reconciliation to God],

24b   Now, to him that is able to keep you from stumbling, and to stand up [Christ Jesus], the very presence of God's unblemished opinion in you,

25a   To God, our Saviour, through Jesus Christ, our Lord, whose wisdom alone [is greater than the wisdom of]

Hod (glory), Malchut (majesty) and Gevurah (dominion), [the left column,

25b   May his] authority [be over] all [worlds], both now, and to all ages. Amen.

(ATB)

THE BOOK OF JUDE

KING JAMES
TRANSLATION

King James Translation

[1] Jude, the servant of Jesus Christ, and brother of James, to them that are sanctified by God the Father, and preserved in Jesus Christ, and called:

[2] Mercy unto you, and peace, and love, be multiplied.

[3] Beloved, when I gave all diligence to write unto you of the common salvation, it was needful for me to write unto you, and exhort you that ye should earnestly contend for the faith which was once delivered unto the saints.

[4] For there are certain men crept in unawares, who were before of old ordained to this condemnation, ungodly men, turning the grace of our God into lasciviousness, and denying the only Lord God, and our Lord Jesus Christ.

[5] I will therefore put you in remembrance, though ye once knew this, how that the Lord, having saved the people out of the land of Egypt, afterward destroyed them that believed not.

[6] And the angels which kept not their first estate, but left their own habitation, he hath reserved in everlasting chains under darkness unto the judgment of the great day.

[7] Even as Sodom and Gomorrah, and the cities about them in like manner, giving themselves over to fornication, and going after strange flesh, are set forth for an example, suffering the vengeance of eternal fire.

[8] Likewise also these filthy dreamers defile the flesh, despise dominion, and speak evil of dignities.

[9] Yet Michael the archangel, when contending with the devil he disputed about the body of Moses, durst not bring

against him a railing accusation, but said, The Lord rebuke thee.

¹⁰ But these speak evil of those things which they know not: but what they know naturally, as brute beasts, in those things they corrupt themselves.

¹¹ Woe unto them! for they have gone in the way of Cain, and ran greedily after the error of Balaam for reward, and perished in the gainsaying of Core.

¹² These are spots in your feasts of charity, when they feast with you, feeding themselves without fear: clouds they are without water, carried about of winds; trees whose fruit withereth, without fruit, twice dead, plucked up by the roots;

¹³ Raging waves of the sea, foaming out their own shame; wandering stars, to whom is reserved the blackness of darkness for ever.

¹⁴ And Enoch also, the seventh from Adam, prophesied of these, saying, Behold, the Lord cometh with ten thousands of his saints,

¹⁵ To execute judgment upon all, and to convince all that are ungodly among them of all their ungodly deeds which they have ungodly committed, and of all their hard speeches which ungodly sinners have spoken against him.

¹⁶ These are murmurers, complainers, walking after their own lusts; and their mouth speaketh great swelling words, having men's persons in admiration because of advantage.

¹⁷ But, beloved, remember ye the words which were spoken before of the apostles of our Lord Jesus Christ;

¹⁸ How that they told you there should be mockers in the last time, who should walk after their own ungodly lusts.

¹⁹ These be they who separate themselves, sensual, having not the Spirit.

[20] But ye, beloved, building up yourselves on your most holy faith, praying in the Holy Ghost,

[21] Keep yourselves in the love of God, looking for the mercy of our Lord Jesus Christ unto eternal life.

[22] And of some have compassion, making a difference:

[23] And others save with fear, pulling them out of the fire; hating even the garment spotted by the flesh.

[24] Now unto him that is able to keep you from falling, and to present you faultless before the presence of his glory with exceeding joy,

[25] To the only wise God our Saviour, be glory and majesty, dominion and power, both now and ever. Amen.

KJV

THE BOOK OF JUDE

ALTERNATE TRANSLATION WORKUP

Alternate Translation Work-Up

Including Translators Notes and Comments

NO NOTES FOR VERSE 1

1 Jude, the servant of Jesus Christ, and brother of James, to them that are sanctified by God the Father, and preserved in Jesus Christ, and called: (KJV)

NO NOTES FOR VERSE 2

[2] Mercy unto you, and peace, and love, be multiplied. (KJV)

VERSE 3

[3] Beloved, **when** I gave all diligence to write unto you of the common salvation, it was needful for me to write unto

you, and exhort you that ye should earnestly contend for the faith which was once delivered unto the saints. (KJV)

NT:2839- Common

2839. **koino/$** *koinós*; fem. *koin¢¡*, neut. *koinón*, adj. Defiled, common, unclean, to lie common or open to all, common or belonging to several or of which several are partakers (Acts 2:44; 4:32; Titus 1:4; Jude 3); unclean hands (Mark 7:2) or meats (Acts 10:14,28; 11:8; Rom 14:14; Heb 10:29, **unconsecrated and therefore having no atoning**

efficacy) such as were common to other nations but were avoided by the Jews as polluted and unclean (Mark 7:2).

(From The Complete Word Study Dictionary: New Testament © 1992 by AMG International, Inc. Revised Edition, 1993)

efficacy

noun, plural **ef·fi·ca·cies.**
capacity for producing a desired result or effect; effectiveness: *a remedy of great efficacy.*

Beloved, it was morally necessary (needful) for me to write to you, to exhort you to seriously strive [to recover] the faith that was given to the Saints at one time, [wherefore], I have made every effort to write to you concerning the salvation that does not produce the atonement (common),

3 Beloved, it was morally necessary for me to write to you, to exhort you to seriously strive [to recover] the faith that was given to the Saints at one time, [wherefore], I have made every effort to write to you concerning the salvation that does not produce the atonement,

(ATB)

COMMENT: **The atonement is Christ Jesus**, the manchild.

The salvation that does not produce the atonement is the salvation of the human spirit.

It is the salvation of the Nefesh that produces the atonement.

Fait, is the virile female seed, either resurrected from the previous age, or received anew from the Lord Jesus Christ.

Rom 5:11

11 AND NOT ONLY SO, BUT WE ALSO JOY IN GOD THROUGH OUR LORD JESUS CHRIST, BY WHOM WE HAVE NOW RECEIVED THE ATONEMENT. (KJV)

NT:2643 - atonement

NT:2643 καταλλαγή **katallage** (kat-al-lag-ay'); from NT:2644; exchange (figuratively, adjustment), i.e. restoration to (the divine) favor:

KJV - atonement, reconciliation (-ing).

(Biblesoft's New Exhaustive Strong's Numbers and Concordance with Expanded Greek-Hebrew Dictionary. Copyright © 1994, 2003, 2006 Biblesoft, Inc. and International Bible Translators, Inc.)

VERSE 4

4 For there are certain men crept in unawares, who were before of old ordained to this condemnation, ungodly men, turning the grace of our God into

lasciviousness, and denying the only Lord God, and our Lord Jesus Christ. (KJV)

To enter secretly (crept in unawares) some (there are certain) man (Strong's 444 = the mature female Adam – Christ Jesus) of olden times refer to the future (were before ordained) to this legal sentence (condemnation) without fear of God (ungodly men) God our acceptance (grace) changing (turning) into insatiable desire for pleasure and the only master (Lord = Strongs's1203) and Lord (Strong's 2962) our Jesus Christ refusing (denying)

17

To enter secretly some man of olden times refer to the future to this legal sentence without fear of God our acceptance changing into insatiable desire for pleasure and the only master and Lord our Jesus Christ refusing

4 [Because] it is written that [in the last days], condemned [souls] from the previous ages, who have no fear of God, will secretly enter into [your subconscious], alongside Adam, [your righteous mind], with the intent of changing [your bodies, that] God' has accepted, into vehicles to satisfy their] insatiable desire for pleasure, and they refuse to honor our only master, God and the Lord Jesus Christ,

(ATB)

VERSE 5

5 I will therefore put you in remembrance, though ye once knew this, how that the Lord, having saved the people out of the land of Egypt, afterward destroyed them that believed not. (KJV)

I will, therefore, remind you of what you once knew, that the Lord, after saving the people out of the land of Egypt, destroyed [their personalities and their bodies], because Christ did not [rise in them, wherefore, there was no female seed to join his male seed to],

5   I will, therefore, remind you of what you once knew, [that when Christ did not rise] in the people after the Lord saved them out of the land of Egypt, [their personalities and their bodies] were destroyed, because the male had no place to attach itself],

(ATB)

COMMENT: The word ***destroyed*** suggests that Jehovah broke down the fallen soul, but was able to extract only the human spirit, his breath, and could not save their personalities/Nefeshot, because Christ did not rise.

So, the destruction was not a punishment. The destruction was a phase of the process of salvation. Their personalities could have been saved if they had chosen Christ over their fallen natures. But, as we find out in verse 9, even Moses did not take the victory.

1 Cor 15:3-5

³ FOR I DELIVERED UNTO YOU FIRST OF ALL THAT WHICH I ALSO RECEIVED, HOW THAT CHRIST DIED FOR OUR SINS ACCORDING TO THE SCRIPTURES;

⁴ AND THAT HE WAS BURIED, AND THAT HE ROSE AGAIN THE THIRD DAY ACCORDING TO THE SCRIPTURES:

⁵ AND THAT HE WAS SEEN OF CEPHAS, THEN OF THE TWELVE: (KJV)

VERSE 6

⁶ And the angels which kept not their first estate, but left their own habitation, he hath reserved in everlasting chains under darkness unto the judgment of the great day. (KJV)

And the Angels which did not guard themselves at their beginning (first estate), but left their own residences, are [now] prisoners, under the judgment of [reincarnation, which] shackles them to the dark under[side of mortal mankind], perpetually, until the great day [of Jubilee, when all will be restored],

6   And the Angels which did not guard themselves at their beginning, but left their own residences, are [now] prisoners under the judgment of [reincarnation, which] shackles

them to the dark under[side of mortal mankind], perpetually, until the great day [of Jubilee, when everything will be restored to its rightful owner]

6   And the Angels which did not guard themselves at their beginning, but left their own residences [to join with the earth, [and] are [now] imprisoned by the legal decree [that] shackles them, to the dark under[side of mortal mankind], [through] perpetual [reincarnations], until the great day [of Jubilee, when everything will be restored to its rightful owner], and

(ATB)

COMMENT: The phrase, ***they left their own residences***, suggests that the fallen Kings departed from their respective Sefirot to join with the earthen layer of the seed of Tevunah, The Sefirot of the Son are attached to the Mother. They were smashed into pieces as the angels of the 7 emotive Sefirot of God sought to transfer their allegiances from Jehovah to the other side, from where they thought they could possess and rule over man, who Elohim clearly declared was to rule over them. (Gen. 1:28)

So the sparks that Rabbi Luria speaks about are actually the fragments of the Sefirot. The ***Names*** associated with the Sefirot, incarnated in the earth as the Kings of Edom, and still exist today as subconscious mental and emotional archetypes in all human beings. (Gen 16:15 -19)

Seven died, that is, the Malchuts of Chesed through Malchut, and one is still alive today, that is the Malchut of the Mother, called, ***the Shekinah in captivity,*** the human spirit.

VERSE 7

⁷ Even as Sodom and Gomorrha and the cities about them gave themselves over to fornication and went after strange flesh, in like manner, these are set forth for an example, suffering the vengeance of eternal fire. (KJV)

Even as Sodom and Gomorrah, and the cities around them, in like manner, these [fallen Kings were] unchaste (giving themselves over to fornication) and going to the back=unconscious mind (after) flesh that was different than theirs (strange) are set forth as examples of the justice of [Binah], the eternal fire, [for those who] do not restrain themselves (vengeance=under)

7   Even as Sodom and Gomorrah and the **cities** around them, were given over to fornication and became the unconscious mind of the flesh [animals, who] were different than them, in like manner, [these fallen Kings are set forth as examples of the justice of [Elohim], the eternal fire, [for those who] do not restrain themselves,

NT:4670 - Sodom

4670. Σόδομα *Sódoma*; gen. *Sodómœn*, neut. pl. proper noun transliterated from the Hebr. *Sedœm* (5467), **burning**.

(from The Complete Word Study Dictionary: New Testament © 1992 by AMG International, Inc. Revised Edition, 1993)

NT:1116 - Gommorah

1116. Γόμορρα *Gómorra*; gen. *Gomórras*, fem. proper noun. Hebr. *'Amœr'h* (6017). Gomorrah meaning **submersion**.

(from The Complete Word Study Dictionary: New Testament © 1992 by AMG International, Inc. Revised Edition, 1993)

John 15:6

6 IF A MAN ABIDE NOT IN ME, HE IS CAST FORTH AS A BRANCH, AND IS WITHERED; AND MEN GATHER THEM, AND CAST THEM INTO THE FIRE, AND THEY ARE BURNED. (KJV)

[These fallen Kings, who] were separated from [Jehovah], their source (Gomorrah), burnt (Sodom) in the [lake] of fire, [Elohim's] justice, [and] attached (fornication) to the flesh of another [species to learn how to put their spiritual] lewdness under [foot], are also set forth as examples

7   [And now we see that these same fallen Kings who] were separated from [Jehovah], their source (Gomorrah), [and who] also came under [Elohim's] justice, [which] burnt (Sodom) [them] in the [lake] of fire, are examples of [Jehovah's judgment upon] lust [for spiritual ascension], which corrupted the flesh of the other [species that] they were attached (fornication) to with lascivious thoughts, and

7   [And now we see that these same fallen Kings who] were separated from [Jehovah], their source (Gomorrah), [and who] also came under [Elohim's] justice, [which] burnt (Sodom) [them] in the [lake] of fire, are examples of [Jehovah's judgment upon] lust [for spiritual ascension], which corrupted the flesh of the other [species that] they were attached to with lascivious thoughts, and

(ATB)

COMMENT: The lust for ascension in the fallen Kings manifested as lust for sex in mankind.

VERSE 8

8 Likewise also these filthy dreamers defile the flesh, despise dominion, and speak evil of dignities. (KJV)

Likewise, indeed, (untranslated) these dreamers also (filthy not in the Greek) pollute (defile) the flesh [animal], indeed (untranslated), they render null and void (despise), indeed, (untranslated) secular authority that promotes liberty (dominion), and slanders (speak evil of) the opinions of God (dignities)

Likewise, indeed, these dreamers also pollute the flesh [animal], indeed, they render null and void, indeed, secular authority that promotes liberty, and slanders the opinions of God

8   Likewise, indeed, these dreamers [of a Utopian society], also pollute the flesh [animals they inhabit], and, indeed, they slander [Christ], the opinion of God, and render secular authority that promotes liberty, null and void, and

8   And, likewise, in the same manner, they, indeed, also pollute your flesh]; indeed, they slander [Christ], the opinion of God, and render secular authority that promotes liberty, null and void, [to bring to pass] their dream [of a one-world Utopian society that they will rule over];

(ATB)

COMMENT: The word *these* is very significant in that it is classic Kabbalah to say that it refers to the sons of God who became the fallen Kings. In addition, the word *dreamer* refers to Joseph, suggesting that these sons who have gone astray are the roots of the spiritual tribe of Joseph, the Viceroy of Egypt.

Gen 37:5-10

5 AND JOSEPH DREAMED A DREAM, AND HE TOLD IT HIS BRETHREN: AND THEY HATED HIM YET THE MORE.

6 AND HE SAID UNTO THEM, HEAR, I PRAY YOU, THIS DREAM WHICH I HAVE DREAMED:

7 FOR, BEHOLD, WE WERE BINDING SHEAVES IN THE FIELD, AND, LO, MY SHEAF AROSE, AND ALSO STOOD UPRIGHT; AND, BEHOLD, YOUR SHEAVES STOOD ROUND ABOUT, AND MADE OBEISANCE TO MY SHEAF.

8 AND HIS BRETHREN SAID TO HIM, SHALT THOU INDEED REIGN OVER US? OR SHALT THOU INDEED HAVE DOMINION OVER US? AND THEY HATED HIM YET THE MORE FOR HIS DREAMS, AND FOR HIS WORDS.

9 AND HE DREAMED YET ANOTHER DREAM, AND TOLD IT HIS BRETHREN, AND SAID, BEHOLD, I HAVE DREAMED A DREAM MORE; AND, BEHOLD, THE SUN and the moon and the eleven stars made obeisance to me.

10 AND HE TOLD IT TO HIS FATHER, AND TO HIS BRETHREN: AND HIS FATHER REBUKED HIM, AND SAID UNTO HIM, WHAT IS THIS DREAM THAT THOU HAST DREAMED? SHALL I AND THY MOTHER AND THY BRETHREN INDEED COME TO BOW DOWN OURSELVES TO THEE TO THE EARTH (KJV)

COMMENT: The significance here is that the fallen kings think they are ordained by God to rule over mankind, just as Joseph's dream predicted that Joseph would rule over Egypt.

VERSE 9

⁹ Yet Michael the archangel, when contending with the devil he disputed about the body of Moses, durst not bring against him a railing accusation, but said, The Lord rebuke thee. (KJV)

Yet, when Michael the Archangel verbally (disputed = speak) distinguished (contending) [between] the devil.[Moses' unrighteous personality, and] Moses' living

[spiritual] body, he dared not bring an official judgment (accusation) of blasphemy (railing) against [Moses], but said, the Lord charges you [with blasphemy]

COMMENT: Michael was afraid to rebuke the fallen Kings because Michael is Christ, the female seed, and the fallen Kings are male.

9   Indeed, when Michael, the Archangel, verbally distinguished [between] the Devil, [the fallen Kings, Moses' emotions, and Christ], Moses' living, [spiritual] body, he dared not bring an official judgment of blasphemy against [the fallen Kings within Moses], but said, the Lord charges you [with blasphemy],

(ATB)

VERSE 10

10 But these speak evil of those things which they know not: but what they know naturally, as brute beasts, in those things they corrupt themselves. (KJV)

But these, as much as (those things which) indeed (untranslated) they do not understand (know) speak evil of Elohim (what), but as physical (naturally) irrational beasts they know how to do the things that [cause Christ] to wither and shrivel up

But these, as much as indeed they do not understand speak evil of Elohim, but as physical irrational beasts they know how to do the things that [cause Christ] to wither and shrivel up

10   But, as much as, indeed, these physical, irrational beasts do not understand that they are speaking evil of Elohim, nevertheless, they know how to do the things that [cause Christ] to wither and shrivel up,

(ATB)

VERSE 11

11 Woe unto them! for they have gone in the way of Cain, and ran greedily after the error of Balaam for reward, and perished in the gainsaying of Core. (KJV)

11   Woe unto them because they are following Cain's lifestyle, and making the same mistakes as Balaam, who hired out his anointing for pay, and Korah, who disputed [Moses' right to rule over Israel],

(ATB)

26

VERSE 12

   12 These are spots in your feasts of charity, when they feast with you, feeding themselves without fear: clouds they are without water, carried about of winds; trees whose fruit withereth, without fruit, twice dead, plucked up by the roots;

   (KJV)

   These are in agape love (feasts of charity) your reef or rocks in the sea (spots) to hold in a good position (when they feast) fearlessly themselves to tend as a shepherd (feeding) clouds waterless of wind to bear alongside (carried about) trees stripped of leaves (whose fruit withereth) barren twice dead uprooted

   These are in agape love your reef or rocks in the sea to hold in a good position fearlessly themselves to tend as a shepherd clouds waterless of wind to bear alongside trees stripped of leaves barren twice dead uprooted

   12   These are the reefs in the sea [that will shipwreck the soul that is born from the] love of God, so hold your [ship] on a good course, and fearlessly teach true doctrine; [and avoid] the souls that have no spirit [in their sails, that] bear alongside [Adam to take his energy]; they are uprooted [spiritual] trees, stripped of [their outer bodies, and] unable to produce others, who died [when they left their primordial residences, and] died again [on the other side of the flood]

   (ATB)

VERSE 13

¹³ Raging waves of the sea, foaming out their own shame; wandering stars, to whom is reserved the blackness of darkness for ever. (KJV)

Waves/curved wild/turbulent/tempestuous (raging) sea to foam up own shame/female organ stars wandering to whom gloom (darkness) for the age

Curved signifies sefirot; bubbling up=incarnation, raging=emotions of the fallen Kings; shame=female organ/mind, reserved=guard from loss or injury, sea= unconscious mind, leviathan is the single name for the 6 Sefirot of ZA, the Son, which is heaven, stars are the Sefirot of heaven

Amos 8:12
¹² AND THEY **SHALL WANDER FROM SEA TO SEA**, AND FROM THE NORTH EVEN TO THE EAST, THEY SHALL RUN TO AND FRO **TO SEEK THE WORD OF THE LORD** , AND SHALL NOT FIND IT.

KJV

2 Tim 3:6
⁶ FOR OF THIS SORT ARE THEY WHICH CREEP INTO HOUSES, AND LEAD CAPTIVE SILLY WOMEN LADEN WITH SINS, LED AWAY WITH DIVERS LUSTS, (KJV)

Wild turbulent Sefirot bubbling up into incarnation from bottom of Satan's sea, the unconscious part of their own female mind, wandering stars, gloomy shadows who guard themselves from loss or injury in this age

Gloomy shadows wandering from sea [to sea, looking for the Word of God from] their own female mind, who guard themselves from loss or injury in this age by incarnating as the wild turbulent [emotions of the male] Sefirot of [Leviathan]

Gloomy shadows wandering from unconscious mind [to unconscious mind, looking for the Word of God from] their own female mind, who guard themselves from loss or injury in this age by incarnating as the wild turbulent [emotions of the male] Sefirot of [Leviathan]

13   Gloomy shadows that wander into the unconscious part of the female mind [with] their own [interpretation of the Scripture], and guard themselves from loss or injury in this age, by incarnating as the wild, turbulent [emotions of Leviathan's male] Sefirot (ATB)

VERSE 14

¹⁴ And Enoch also, the seventh from Adam, prophesied of these, saying, Behold, the Lord cometh with ten thousands of his saints, (KJV)

OT:2585 - Enoch

OT:2585   חֲנוֹךְ **Chanowk** (khan-oke'); from **OT:2596**; **initiated**;   Chanok,   an   antediluvian   patriach:

KJV - Enoch.

OT:2596

OT:2596 חָנַךְ **chanak** (khaw-nak'); a primitive root; properly, to narrow (compare OT:2614); figurative-ly, **to initiate or discipline**:

KJV - dedicate, train up.

(Biblesoft's New Exhaustive Strong's Numbers and Concordance with Expanded Greek-Hebrew Dictionary. Copyright © 1994, 2003, 2006 Biblesoft, Inc. and International Bible Translators, Inc.)

COMMENT: Enoch is the Shekinah in captivity, the eighth King of Edom.

Gen 5:24
24 AND ENOCH WALKED WITH GOD: AND HE WAS NOT; FOR GOD TOOK HIM. (KJV)

Enoch was not raptured. He was joined, or rejoined, to Jehovah, just as the Lord Jesus, after him, was joined to Jehovah.

Abel died and Cain knew his wife and reproduced. Repentance came forth in Lamech. After that Abel rose to the surface again, and Cain and Abel together are called Adam.

Lamech is the last named person in Cain's line, because after that, humanity is remembered through Seth, Adam's new righteous seed.

The names are similar, because this was a new start.

Enoch was the seventh Sefirah of the renewed Adam, and when he comes together with the souls of Christ Jesus in the Body of Christ, which is Noah, 10,000, the number of Chochmah, the 2nd Sefirah of Adam, comes into existence, and brings judgment on all ungodliness from that high place, which is total destruction of the fallen soul. This is the breaking of the soul into pieces. The spirit is saved. If Christ Jesus is present, the personality is saved. If not, the personality dies.

14   And Enoch, [the disciplinarian], the 7th [Sefirah] of Adam, prophesied of these, saying, behold, [when] the Lord comes [together with] the Saints, wisdom (10,000)

(ATB)

VERSE 15

15 To execute judgment upon all, and to convince all that are ungodly among them of all their ungodly deeds which they have ungodly committed, and of all their hard speeches which ungodly sinners have spoken against him. (KJV)

To judge [if] the whole [Adam is present] and to convince all souls of all their ungodly actions wicked (they have committed) and of all their unanointed (dry) [words] they have spoken against themselves (him) wicked (ungodly)

To judge [if] the whole [Adam is present] and to convince all souls of all their ungodly actions wicked and of all their unanointed [words] they have spoken against themselves wicked

15   To judge the whole [Adam is present], and to convince all their souls of all [their] ungodly actions, and of all the wicked, carnal [words that their] wicked [selves] have spoken against their [righteous] selves,

(ATB)

VERSE 16

16 These are murmurers, complainers, walking after their own lusts; and their mouth speaketh great swelling words, having men's persons in admiration because of advantage. (KJV)

And [the bodies that these are incarnate in], are grumblers (murmurers) discontented (complainers) walking after their own lusts, and their mouths speaking pride fully, and flattering people for their benefit

16   And [the bodies that these fallen Kings are incarnate in], are discontented, grumblers, whose mouths speak prideful [words] that flatter people for their own benefit, [whose main purpose in life is] to satisfy their own lusts,

(ATB)

VERSE 17

¹⁷ But, beloved, remember ye the words which were spoken before of the apostles of our Lord Jesus Christ; (KJV)

17   Indeed, beloved of God, you should remember the predictions of the apostles of the Lord Jesus Christ,

(ATB)

VERSE 18

¹⁸ How that they told you there should be mockers in the last time, who should walk after their own ungodly lusts. (KJV)

18   How they told you that in the last days, there would be false teachers who would follow after their own ungodly lusts [to teach, rather than the Spirit of Truth], and

(ATB)

VERSE 19

¹⁹ These be they who separate themselves, sensual, having not the Spirit. (KJV)

19   That there would be those who would hold onto their bestial nature (sensual) and refuse to separate it from the Spirit [of Truth],

19   That there would be those who would hold onto their bestial nature and refuse to separate it from the Spirit [of Truth],

(ATB)

VERSE 20

²⁰ But ye, beloved, building up yourselves on your most holy faith, praying in the Holy Ghost, (KJV)

20   But you, beloved of God, are rearing up (building up) [Christ Jesus], the holy one, upon [the foundation of] your faith, [which you received by] praying in the Holy Spirit

COMMENT: The Holy Spirit provides the female seed, which is our faith.

20 But you, beloved of God, are rearing up [Christ Jesus], the holy one, upon [the foundation of] your faith, [which you received by] praying in the Holy Spirit,

(ATB)

VERSE 21

21 Keep yourselves in the love of God, looking for the mercy of our Lord Jesus Christ unto eternal life. (KJV)

21 So, let the love of God guard you against loss or injury [in this age] by looking for the mercy of our Lord Jesus Christ, unto eternal life, and

(ATB)

VERSE 22

22 And of some have compassion, making a difference: (KJV)

22 On some have compassion and thoroughly separate [their bestial nature from the Spirit of Truth], and

(ATB)

VERSE 23

23 And others save with fear, pulling them out of the fire; hating even the garment spotted by the flesh. (KJV)

23   And others save by pulling them out of the fire; and, in indeed, be compassionate (untranslated word 1653), but be careful (fear) that that which is detestable does not stain the flesh of your body (garment);

23   And others save by pulling them out of the fire; and, indeed, be compassionate, but be careful that, that which is detestable does not stain the flesh of your body;

(ATB)

VERSE 24

[24] Now unto him that is able to keep you from falling, and to present you faultless before the presence of his glory with exceeding joy, (KJV)

24   Now, to him that is able to keep you from stumbling (falling) and to stand up (present) his very presence opinion (glory) be unblemished (faultless) with exuberant joy

24   Now, to him that is able to keep you from stumbling, and to stand up the very presence of his unblemished opinion in you with exuberant joy,

(ATB)

VERSE 25

[25] To the only wise God our Saviour, be glory and majesty, dominion and power, both now and ever. Amen. (KJV)

25 To be only wise God Savior through (not translated) our Jesus Christ our Lord (not translated) opinion (glory) strength/greatness (majesty) strength (dominion) and

authority (power) for all (ever) age (untranslated) both now and toward whole (all) (untranslated) age (ever). Amen.

COMMENT: the words *through Jesus Christ our Lord* are in the Greek, but are not translated because the whole sentence reveals the truth, that Jesus is not God. He is the Son of God, God's Name, in the same manner that Joseph wielded all the power of Pharaoh in Egypt.

Jehovah, God, is the savior. Jesus is the savior of the body that he dwells in through his son, Christ Jesus.

To the only wise **God, our Savior, through** Jesus Christ our Lord

Jehovah is God and Christ our Lord, the controller of our sin nature.

25   To God, our Saviour, through Jesus Christ, our Lord, whose wisdom alone [is greater than], Hod (glory) Malchut (majesty) and Gevurah (dominion), [the whole left column, who has] authority [over] all [worlds], both now, and to all ages. Amen.

(ATB)

Table of References

Recommended Additional Study

The following Christ-Centered Kabbalah Messages are recommended for whoever might be interested in a deeper understanding of Jude's message to the Israel of God:

803 – The Pharisees & The Widow

ABOUT THE AUTHOR

Sheila R. Vitale is the Spiritual Leader, Founding Teacher, and Pastor of Living Epistles Ministries (*LEM*) and Christ-Centered Kabbalah (*CCK*). A brief history of Pastor Vitale and the unique two-pronged ministry that the Lord Jesus Christ gave her charge over (*LEM/CCK*) is encapsulated below

She moves in the offices of Teacher of Apostolic Doctrine, Prophet, Evangelist and Pastor, has an international following, and has been expounding on the Scripture through a unique spiritual lens for nearly three decades. She has written more than 50 books based on the Old and New Testaments including *The Kabbalah of The 1ˢᵗ Epistle of John* and *the Crime of the Calf* (OT) and *The Three Israels* and *Jesus and The Learned Jew* (NT*)*. She has also rendered original spiritual interpretations of Biblical texts such as *The Prophesies of Daniel According to Kabbalah, Chapter 11,* and *The Noah Chronicles*. Her unique, Multi-Part Message style is seen in *CCK* Serial Messages such as Reincarnation vs Transmigration (22 Parts) and Exodus, Chapter 32 (26 Parts). Each Part of a Multi-Part Message Series can also be enjoyed as a complete and independent study. In addition, she has defined, explained, illustrated and demonstrated hundreds of spiritual principles throughout more than 1,000 CCK lectures.

Her signature work, however, is the three volumes of *The Alternate Translation Bible (ATB)*: *The Alternate Translation Of The Old Testament*, *The Alternate Translation of the New Testament* and *The Alternate Translation of The Book of Revelation*. *The Alternate Translation Bible* is a work in progress (*The ATB Project*). Accordingly, additional spiritual interpretations of both whole and partial Chapters are added from time to time, as they are rendered. The most up-to-date versions of *The ATB Project* may be found online at the *LEM and CCK* websites: *LivingEpistles.org and Christ-CenteredKabbalah.org*, respectively. *The ATB* is a *spiritual interpretation* of the Scripture and is not intended to replace traditional translations.

41

She also analyzed the Greek text of The Book of Revelation and preached extensively on it in the early years of The ATB Project. During that time she produced 197 distinct Message Parts, under 29 specific Message Titles, all of which deal with The Book of Revelation.

Pastor Vitale is an illustrator of spiritual principles, a researcher, a translator and a reviewer of the Modern Social Trends of Family and Culture, as they are revealed through TV programs (*The Sopranos),* movies (*The Matrix* and *The Edge of Tomorrow)*, and plays (*Wicked)*. She also writes for the CCK *Blog.*

She travels domestically, as well as internationally, preaching and teaching Judeo-Christian Spiritual Philosophy, and has donated Audio Message Libraries of her Lectures to ministries in Asia, Africa, Europe and North America.

Pastor Vitale serves *CCK* in a range of spiritual, educational, and administrative functions from *The Selden Centre, LEM/CCK* headquarters in Selden, New York. She is also a philanthropic individual who supports the *Lighthouse Mission (Patchogue, NY) and HGM – Mission of Hope – Haiti, and other* charitable organizations. She also supports community services such as the *Terryville Fire Department.*

In her spare time, Pastor Vitale enjoys watching movies, attending plays and partaking of cuisines from different cultures. An avid traveler, she has visited several countries in Europe and Africa as well as many cities in the United States.

BEGINNINGS, INSPIRATION AND CALLING

Pastor Vitale began her spiritual journey as a child when her Jewish mother enrolled her in the Hebrew school of an Orthodox synagogue. She experienced the Spirit of God for the first time there in such a profound way that she wept. But after that, when she was only eleven years old, she became very ill and was taken to Mount Sinai Hospital in New York City. She almost died there and has battled with life-threatening health issues ever since. Nevertheless, a deep longing for God continued to pursue her until several years later when she desperately wanted to attend Yeshiva (Jewish high school), but could not. Her secular parents approved of her choice but were not able to afford the tuition.

Much later, after years of searching, she once again experienced the Spirit that had brought her to tears in the synagogue of her youth, but this time it was at *Gospel Revivals Ministries*, a Pentecostal church where Deliverance Ministry was emphasized. She desired to understand the Bible since she was a child, but Scripture was difficult for her and she struggled with the text. Nevertheless, she read one Chapter of the Bible every day until, one day, *her spiritual eyes opened* and she saw an angel holding a little book.

After that, she attended as many as five teaching services each week for about seven years, the latter part of which she edited *Pastor Holzhauser's* books. But several more years had to pass before *the eyes of her understanding opened even further* and she began to receive *Revelation Knowledge of the Scripture*. She understood at that time that the angel she had seen was the angel of Revelation 10:8.

After about seven years of learning *Deliverance Ministry* and *The Doctrine of Sonship* (*Bill Britton*) from *Pastor Holzhauser,* she studied the Bible independently under the influence and direction of the Holy Spirit.

In **1988** she began teaching Apostolic Doctrine.

In **1990** she spent three months in Stony Brook Hospital where she recovered from an incurable disease, defeating premature death, once again, and went on to resume teaching and managing *LEM*.

In **1992** she journeyed to Africa for the first time where she was called to the office of Evangelist.

In the **mid-1990s,** she began to Pastor in addition to being a Teacher of Apostolic Doctrine, a Prophet and an Evangelist, thus, satisfying all five offices of *The Ministry of the Lord Jesus Christ to His Church.*

LIVING EPISTLES MINISTRIES

Pastor Vitale was happy fellowshipping at *Gospel Revivals Ministries* but, eventually, she desired a deeper and more spiritual understanding of the Word of God. One day, after crying out to Jesus about her need, she was amazed to hear Him ask her if she would teach. Her initial response was that she did not see how it would be possible since she was already working a full-time job, despite her poor health. But after the Lord asked her for a second and then a third time, she reluctantly agreed, believing that He would empower her to do the job. Shortly thereafter, in the latter part of 1987, she began to teach her own brand of Judeo-Christian Spiritual Philosophy.

The Lord Jesus Christ named the work *Living Epistles Ministries* in 1988.

The first *LEM* meetings were casual and spontaneous gatherings of friends and fellow deliverance workers in Pastor Vitale's home. After that, they were held in the business office of one of the brethren. Pastor Vitale delivered her first formal message entitled *The Truth About Witchcraft in January of 1988,* followed by *The Seduction of Eve* in April of the same year. After that, she prepared and taught weekly messages including *Signs of Apostleship* and *Lazarus & The Rich Man. The meetings eventually* increased to two and then three each week.

Sometime after that, she learned that the Lord Jesus Christ was revealing spiritual principles from the Hebrew text of the Old Testament through her teachings, and those spiritual principles helped her to begin to unlock the mysteries of the New Testament, as well. Today she understands that the

Scripture is a spiritual document that must be spiritually discerned if it is to be understood correctly, and calls that spiritual understanding **The Doctrine of Christ**.

CHRIST-CENTERED KABBALAH

Another Beginning

After about ten years of teaching *the Doctrine of Christ*, in or about the year 2000, while she was evangelizing in Greenville, South Carolina, the Lord Jesus Christ introduced Pastor Vitale to *Lurian Kabbalah*. At that time, the Spirit of God directed her to read and study the teachings of *Rabbi Luria*, as written by his student, *Chayyim Vital,* in *The Tree of Life: The Palace of Adam Kadmon*. She did not understand the text at first, but continued on, nevertheless, until *the eyes of her understanding opened*.

Shortly thereafter, she began to teach *Lurian Kabbalah* and eventually applied the spiritual principles of that system to her studies in the Old Testament under the *Living Epistles Ministries* brand. Sometime in or about the year 2001, however, the Lord Jesus Christ named her, then current teachings, Christ-centered Kabbalah (*CCK*), thereby dividing *Living Epistles Ministries* into two branches, each with its own website and digital representations. Each ministry has its own label, but both also share the *LEM/CCK* moniker.

About CCK

Christ-Centered Kabbalah is a new, vigorous approach to spiritual maturity, ascension and rectification (justification) based on Pastor Vitale's original research in *the Hebrew text of the Torah, the Greek text of the New Testament* and *the Zohar*, one of the foundational books of *Philosophical Kabbalah*.

CCK, an integration of the *Doctrine of Christ* and *Lurian Kabbalah*, two Bible-based philosophical systems, offers a fresh perspective concerning Israel's resurrection and Adam's restoration to a higher estate than the one he fell from.

She has studied the authentic Jewish Kabbalah of several Rabbinic scholars, including *Moses Nachmanides (Ramban), Moses Cordovero (Ramak)* and *Isaac Luria (The Ari) and* has read many of the English translations of their writings, including *Ramban's The Gate of Reward, Ramak's Pardes Rimonim (Orchard of Pomegranates)*, and *the* teachings *of the Ari*, as written by his student, *Chayyim Vital: The Gate of Reincarnations* and *The Tree of Life: The Palace of Adam Kadmon.* Pastor Vitale attributes her ability to understand and teach authentic *Jewish Kabbalah* and *Christ-Centered Kabbalah,* which she believes is beyond the grasp of the human mind, to *The Lord Jesus Christ.*

Pastor Vitale cautions her students about the dangers of *Occult Qabalah* and warns everyone with ears to hear that all Kabbalah is not kosher (authentic). Pastor Vitale teaches *authentic Jewish Kabbalah, which glorifies God* and shuns the *occult Qabalah of personal power*, which, all too frequently, is used to control unsuspecting persons, acquire wealth by spiritual power, or punish one's enemies.

Media

CCK publishes a wide range of material, including books, e-books, spiritual interpretations of the Scripture and transcripts of Pastor Vitale's *Christ-Centered Kaballah* Lectures. Many of her transcripts and the entire *Alternate Translation Bible* may be viewed without charge on the *CCK Website* (*Christ-CenteredKaballah.org*).

She also has an *Author's Website* where all of her books, as well as several photographs of herself and a short biography are displayed (Amazon.com/author/SheilaVitale). Paperback and digital versions of *CCK* books may be purchased through *Amazon*, *Google Books* and *Barnes & Noble*. *CCK* also provides free videos of her live streams through YouTube: *@Christ-CenteredKabbalah),* and other Internet Plat-forms.

PASTOR VITALE TODAY

Today Pastor Vitale continues to dedicate her life to teaching the spiritual principles of the Bible and focuses daily on studying, writing and preaching powerful messages from *The Selden Centre,* LEM/CCK's headquarters at Selden, New York.

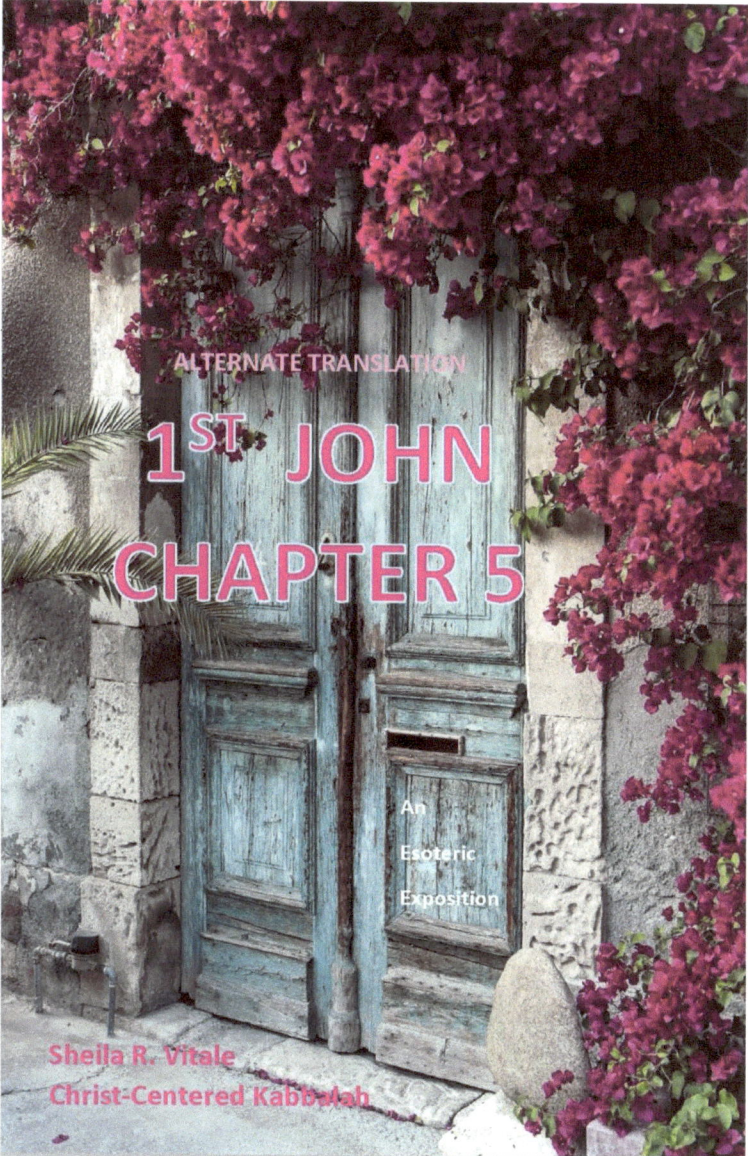

ALTERNATE TRANSLATION

1ST JOHN
CHAPTER 5

An
Esoteric
Exposition

Sheila R. Vitale
Christ-Centered Kabbalah

The Kabbalah of

The First Epistle of John

Chapter 5

An Esoteric Exposition

Sheila Vitale

Christ-Centered Kabbalah

SOPHIA

EXPERIENCING 2ND THESSALONIANS, CHAPTER 2

SHEILA R. VITALE

LIVING EPISTLES MINISTRIES

THE CRIME OF
THE CALF

Sheila R. Vitale   Christ-Centered Kabbalah

The Noah Chronicles

An Esoteric Exposition of Noah's Seduction

Including the Alternate Translation of

Genesis 9:18-27

Sheila R. Vitale

Christ-Centered Kabbalah

CORINTHIAN CONFUSION

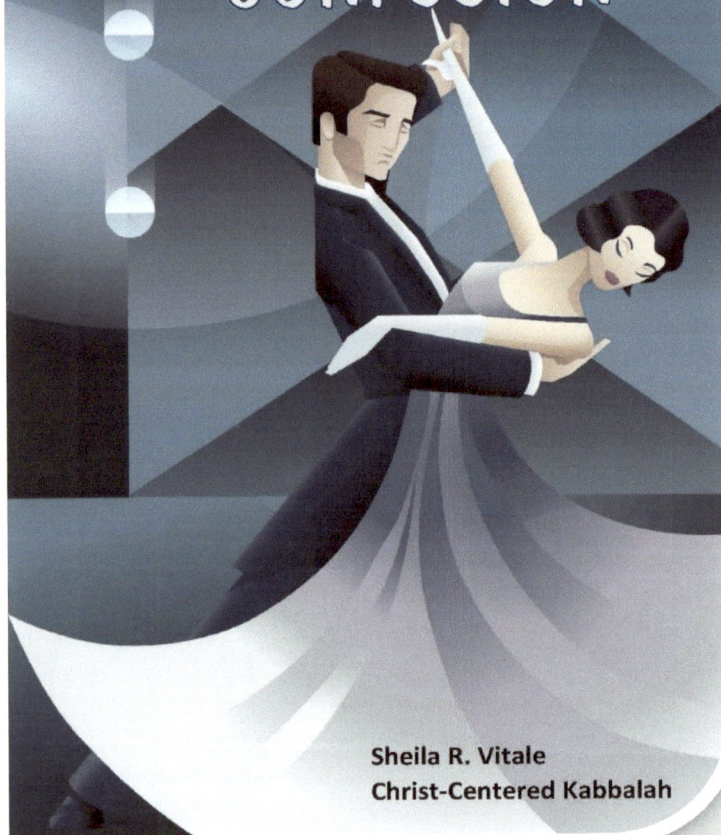

Sheila R. Vitale
Christ-Centered Kabbalah

Christ-Centered Kabbalah
Sheila R Vitale,
Pastor, Teacher & Founder
~ The Compleat Kabbalah ~
PO Box 562, Port Jefferson Station, New York 11776, USA
Christ-CenteredKabbalah.org *or* Books@Christ-CenteredKabbalah.org